PLAY LIKE THE PROS

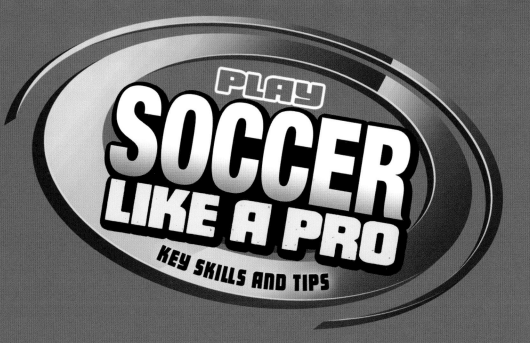

PLAY

SOCCER
LIKE A PRO

KEY SKILLS AND TIPS

BY CHRISTOPHER FOREST

Consultant:
Jeffrey L. Chambers
Head Athletic Trainer
Minnesota State University
Mankato, Minnesota

CAPSTONE PRESS
a capstone imprint

Sports Illustrated KIDS Play Like the Pros is published by Capstone Press,
1710 Roe Crest Drive, North Mankato, Minnesota 56003.
www.capstonepub.com

112018
001226

Books published by Capstone Press are manufactured with paper
containing at least 10 percent post-consumer waste.

Library of Congress Cataloging-in-Publication Data
Forest, Christopher.
    Play soccer like a pro: key skills and tips / By Christopher Forest.
    p. cm.—(Sports illustrated kids : play like the pros)
    Includes bibliographical references and index.
    Summary: "Provides instructional tips on how to improve one's
soccer skills, including quotes and advice from professional coaches and
athletes"—Provided by publisher.
    ISBN 978-1-4296-4827-1 (library binding)
    ISBN 978-1-4296-5647-4 (paperback)
1. Soccer—Training—Juvenile literature. I. Title. II. Series.
GV943.25.F68 2011
796.334071—dc22   2010007244

EDITORIAL CREDITS

Aaron Sautter and Anthony Wacholtz, editors; Ted Williams, designer;
Eric Gohl, media researcher; Laura Manthe, production specialist

PHOTO CREDITS

Shutterstock/hanzl, cover, 3 (soccer ball); kentoh, design element;
    Vjom, design element
Sports Illustrated/Al Tielemans, 21; Bob Martin, 7 (top), 9 (all), 13 (top),
    15, 18 (bottom), 27; Bob Rosato, 19; Damian Strohmeyer, 16; David E.
    Klutho, 7 (bottom); John W. McDonough, 11 (top), 14; Robert Beck, 6,
    24, 29; Simon Bruty, cover (left & right), 4–5, 8, 10, 11 (bottom), 12, 13
    (bottom), 17 (all), 18 (top), 20, 22, 23, 25, 26

TABLE OF CONTENTS

TIPS ▶

▼ FEATURE

SHOOT TO SCORE!

Soccer started with a ball made from animal skin filled with hair. Over thousands of years, both the ball and the sport gradually changed into the game we know today.

Soccer is enjoyed by millions of fans around the world. They love watching Major League Soccer and World Cup matches. With huge stars like David Beckham, Landon Donovan, and Kaká, soccer has become the world's most popular sport.

The stars use kicks, spins, and slide tackles to win games and thrill the fans. But even the biggest stars had to start somewhere. Soccer can be played by people of any age. Patience and a lot of practice are the keys to growing as a soccer player. With a little hard work, you can learn to play soccer just like the professionals.

7 HOW TO DRIBBLE

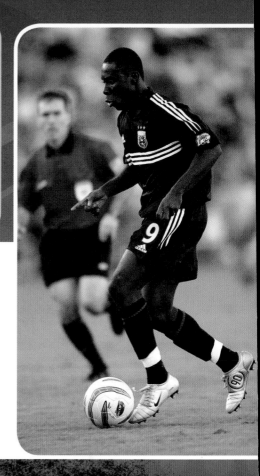

Controlling the soccer ball is the most important skill for any soccer player. Maintaining ball control while racing past the competition can be tricky. But by following these steps, you'll find yourself in total control.

KEEP IT CLOSE

Stay in contact with the ball. As long as you have the ball, be sure to control it between your feet at all times. Defenders will have a hard time stealing the ball if you keep it under control.

"I love having the ball at my feet and running at the defender one-on-one. That's when I'm at my best, when I can pull some weird move and get by him."
-FREDDY ADU, STRIKER, ARIS THESSALONIKI FC

BE LOOSE

To keep defenders off balance, stand with your shoulders slightly lowered. This **stance** helps confuse defenders about which direction you might move. It also forces them to stay back from the ball. Constant movement helps confuse defenders too, so be sure to keep moving on the field.

STAY ALERT

Watch where you're going. Hold your head up and try to stay parallel to the goal lines. Watch the field for an opening, and you'll be prepared to make a play as you dribble.

You dash down the field with the ball at your feet. Suddenly, a defender appears in front of you and tries to steal the ball. In a split second, you have to pass the ball to a teammate. Practice these moves and you'll soon be making dazzling passes.

PLANT IT

Your **plant foot** is very important. Place your plant foot next to the ball as you prepare to make the pass.

TAKE AIM

Aim your kicking foot at the middle of the ball. You'll have better control and the pass will be more accurate.

PUSH IT

Use the inside of your foot to kick the ball. Using the inside of your foot helps keep the ball on the ground. Be certain to follow through with your kicking leg. This method is usually the best way to make a clean pass to your teammate.

Sometimes you need to stop the ball in its tracks. This is called trapping. The best way to trap a ball is to keep your hips facing the ball and your foot loose. When the ball reaches you, put your foot down lightly to slow it down and stop it. Don't stomp down hard or the ball may bounce off in another direction. If all goes well, you'll have the ball trapped so you can easily pass it to your teammate.

▼ Trapping with Your Feet

3 HOW TO MAKE AN ASSIST

You're avoiding defenders as you dribble the ball down the field. Then you spot your teammate cutting toward the goal. It's up to you to make the perfect pass that leads to a score. What you do next might help win the game.

BE AWARE

Always know where your teammates are on the field. Hold your head up so you can see who has the best chance of scoring.

TIME IT RIGHT

Timing your pass correctly is crucial. Be sure to turn and face your open teammate. Then quickly kick the ball so your teammate can get it before the defenders do.

AIM YOUR PASS

Try to aim your pass where only your teammate can get the ball. You don't want your teammate to have to slow down to get it. Keep the ball in front of your teammate so he or she is less likely to lose it.

"For the ideal assist situation, you should buy your teammate some time ... release the ball soon enough so that your teammate is not offsides."
-ALY WAGNER, MIDFIELDER, U.S. NATIONAL TEAM

HOW TO LEGALLY SLIDE TACKLE

Your opponent is making a break for the net. You only have a few seconds to stop him. All you can do is kick the ball away before he makes his shot. To save the game, you may have to make a slide tackle. Here's how to do it the right way.

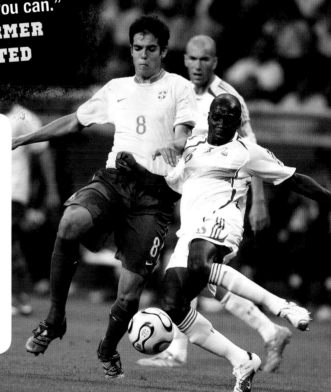

"Tackle standing up first. Avoid going to the ground if you can."
-EDDIE POPE, FORMER PLAYER, D.C. UNITED

THE APPROACH

First run toward your opponent while keeping an eye on the ball. Be sure to note the direction your opponent is going. Then make your move to cut off your opponent's path.

HIT THE DECK

If you need to,
slide on the ground
when you're ready to
kick the ball. Keep
your **cleats** away from the ball as you approach.
It's best to attack the ball head-on or from the side.

MAKE YOUR KICK

As you reach the ball, try to kick it away from
your opponent. Make sure you kick the ball and not
the opposing player. If you contact the opposing
player, you will be charged with a penalty. Then the
other team will be awarded a penalty kick.

5 HOW TO BEAT A DEFENDER

You're controlling the ball, but defenders are trying to steal it away from you. If you can get past them, it's smooth sailing to the goal. But how? If done right, these tips should help you steer clear of determined opponents.

BE ON GUARD

Keep track of your opponents at all times. If you know where the defenders are, you'll have more success at keeping the ball away from them.

FAKE OUT THE DEFENDER

Shoulder **feints** are a great way to keep defenders off balance. Maintain eye contact with your opponent. When you get close, drop one shoulder and pretend to quickly move in one direction. When the defender tries to cut you off, you go in the other direction instead. This move should fake out your opponent, leaving you open to move toward the goal.

USE A SIDE STEP

A side step can also help you avoid an attacker. As the defender closes in, place your foot next to the ball. Just as the attacker gets to you, sweep your foot under the ball. Then push off with your planted foot and run down the field with the ball. The defender will be left trying to change direction while you are long gone.

6 HOW TO MAKE A POWER SHOT

As you run down the field, you find an open shot at the goal. The only thing between you and the net is the goalkeeper. Use these steps to make a powerful shot against the goalie.

POWER YOUR SHOT

Run hard toward the ball as you prepare to kick it. The extra speed will add power to your shot.

THE RIGHT POSITION

As you make your kick, place your plant foot next to the ball. Be sure your plant foot also points toward the goal. Your chest should be positioned directly over the ball.

BOOT IT

Swing your kicking foot down hard to strike the ball. Angle your foot so your shoelaces make contact with the ball. Be sure to follow through with your kick to give it extra power.

David Beckham had to work hard to become a soccer star. While growing up, Beckham was one of the smaller players on the field. He tried to bulk up, but he had trouble gaining muscle in his teenage years. Some coaches thought Beckham was too small to play soccer. But he didn't let that stop him. He played with older players and gained experience playing against his father's friends. In time, he proved he had what it takes to become a superstar.

7 HOW TO MAKE AN ACCURATE SHOT

You're all alone in front of the net. You have a chance to score. But simply kicking the ball won't put it in the net. You need to make the perfect shot against the goalie. Practice these steps to help increase your accuracy.

APPROACH WITH CARE

As you prepare to shoot, place your plant foot 2 to 3 feet (0.6 to 0.9 meter) away from the ball. This position will help you kick with maximum power.

AIM CAREFULLY

For an accurate shot, you need to pick a spot in the net, then position your body correctly. As you make your kick, position your chest and chin over the ball. You should also lock the ankle of your kicking foot to make sure the ball goes where you aim.

FIRE AWAY

It's time to make your move. For the best accuracy, kick the ball with the inside of your foot near the arch. For the most power and speed, be sure to kick the middle part of the ball.

"When kicking the ball, you want to kick the middle of the ball, which generates the most pace. That's what we call the sweet spot."
— EDDIE JOHNSON, STRIKER, KANSAS CITY WIZARDS

8 HOW TO STOP A SHOT

You're alone at the net when an opponent approaches with the ball. As the goalie, you're the only one who can stop the shot. A split second and a fast move could mean the difference between making a save or losing the game. Follow these quick steps to make a game-saving block.

PAY ATTENTION

Stay on the balls of your feet so you can react quickly and easily. Be sure to keep your head up so you can see your opponent. Stay aware of the angle your opponent is taking to make the shot.

GET IN THE AIR

When you go to block the ball, jump in the air. Be sure to time your move just right. Reach your hands up in the air and keep them close together. Blocking the opponent's shot is great. But it's even better if you can catch the ball.

BLOCK IT DOWN

Try to keep your hands above the ball when it's coming at you. This position helps keep the ball down when you stop it. It also reduces the risk of a **rebound** going into the net.

As a goalkeeper, getting the ball to your teammate is essential. The over-arm throw is the goalkeeper's best friend. To do this move, keep your arms straight with your elbows slightly bent. Bring the ball back over your shoulders. Lean forward, then snap your arms forward and release the ball quickly. The goal is to send it to a teammate on one side of the field. This way, the ball will stay far away from the net. It also keeps the opposing team from getting an easy score.

The Over-Arm Throw

↳ rebound—when the ball bounces off the goal or goalkeeper and returns into play

HOW TO THROW IN

The ball goes out of bounds and it's your turn to throw it in. You want to throw the ball so your teammates can get it before the opposing team does. Launch the perfect throw-in with these easy steps.

FANCY FOOTWORK

For a short throw, keep your feet close together and flat on the ground. If you need to throw long, take a few steps behind the sidelines. Then step into your throw. Be careful to keep your feet behind the sidelines and on the ground. Both feet must be in contact with the ground until the ball has left your fingertips. Otherwise, the opposing team will be awarded the throw-in from the same spot.

HOLD ON

Hold the ball firmly with both hands. As you grip the ball, pull it back over your head. Keep your elbows pointed out and your palms behind the ball. The ball must be thrown with both hands over your head, or it will be ruled an illegal throw-in. The opposing team will then be given the throw-in from the same spot.

AIM IT RIGHT

Power your throw with your elbows. This helps keep the ball on target. For longer throws, use your shoulders to power your throw. Always try to aim toward your teammates' feet.

10 HOW TO DEFEND A SHOT

An opposing player races down the field with the ball. He plans to make a shot on your goalie. You're in a position to stop him. What should you do? Use these moves and you could save the day.

KNOW YOUR OPPONENT

The best defense against attackers is to learn about them. What kinds of moves do they like to use? Do they like to take shots on their own? Or do they like to pass to their teammates? By knowing your opponents, you can be prepared for their moves.

STOP THE DRIBBLE

Does your opponent like to dribble? If so, move in close so he or she has to pass the ball.

STOP THE PASS

Does your opponent prefer to pass to a teammate? If so, stay on your toes. Drop back and try to block the **passing lane**. Get in the way and make it difficult for your opponent to pass easily.

↳ **passing lane**—an opening used to pass the ball to another player

77 HOW TO HEAD THE BALL

The ball is in the air. You can see a clear path to the goal. The best chance to score is by making a **header**. It's a useful skill for any soccer player. Practice these tips and you'll soon be making fantastic head shots.

KEEP YOUR EYES ON IT

For a great head shot, keep your eyes on the ball. By watching the ball, you'll be certain to hit the mark. Watching the ball's movement will also help you correctly position your body underneath it.

↳ header—when the head is used to hit the ball

HEADS UP

Just before the ball arrives, pull your head back slightly. When you're ready to make your shot, thrust your head forward and strike the ball with your forehead. Be sure to hit it hard to give the ball some zip.

PROTECT YOURSELF

As you make your shot, keep your arms lifted and parallel to your shoulders. This stance keeps other players away and helps protect you from head-to-head contact.

"[Your forehead] is the hardest part of your head and you get the most power."
— TAYLOR TWELLMAN, FORWARD, NEW ENGLAND REVOLUTION

HOW TO TAKE FREE KICKS

The game is on the line. One of the opposing players is called for a penalty. Now you get to take a free kick for a chance to win the game. Here's how you can get the ball into the net.

CHECK YOUR SPOT

Before you take your shot, check for a good spot to place the ball. Make sure the surface is level and clean. Flat ground will help the ball stay where you put it.

CHECK THE GOALIE

Look to see where the goalie is standing. For the best chance to score, you'll want to aim toward the corner of the goal farthest from the goalie. The corners are usually the hardest spots for the goalie to defend.

"[When free kicking] I like to strike the side of the ball with just the instep of my toe."
— DAVID BECKHAM,
MIDFIELDER, L.A. GALAXY

FIRE AWAY

Kick the ball as hard as you can. Be sure to hit the ball in the "sweet spot." You want as much power and speed as possible to get the ball past the goalie.

Becoming a professional soccer player like David Beckham or Cristiano Ronaldo requires a lot of hard work. To become a complete player, you need to learn a variety of skills. But with some patience and a lot of practice, you can play just like the pros.

GLOSSARY

ATTACKER—a player who tries to score a goal

CLEATS—small rubber or metal studs found on the bottom of soccer shoes; cleats help players gain better footing on the field

DEFENDER—a player who tries to prevent a goal from being scored

FEINT—a fake move used to confuse an opponent

FREE KICK—a kick a team receives as a result of a penalty

HEADER—a move in which a player uses his or her forehead to hit the ball

PASSING LANE—an opening on the field through which a player can pass the ball to a teammate

PLANT FOOT—the foot used to push off from while kicking the ball

REBOUND—when the ball bounces off the goal or goalkeeper and returns into play

SIDE STEP—to move away from a defender or attacker while moving the ball down the field

STANCE—the position of a player's feet and body

READ MORE

Cloake, Martin. *Soccer: The Ultimate Guide.* New York: DK Publishing, 2008.

Crisfield, Deborah W. *The Everything Kids' Soccer Book: Rules, Techniques, and More About Your Favorite Sport!* Avon, Mass.: Adams Media, 2009.

Roselius, J. Chris. *Soccer Skills: How to Play Like a Pro.* How to Play Like a Pro. Berkeley Heights, N.J.: Enslow Publishers, 2009.

INTERNET SITES

FactHound offers a safe, fun way to find Internet sites related to this book. All of the sites on FactHound have been researched by our staff.

Here's all you do:

Visit *www.facthound.com*

Type in this code: 9781429648271

INDEX